The Cirencester Ex[

by

Miriam Harrison & Shirley Alexander

Spital Gate - Cirencester

Published by
REARDON PUBLISHING
56, Upper Norwood Street, Leckhampton,
Cheltenham, Glos, GL53 0DU

Copyright ©1998
A joint publication between
Reardon Publishing and Corinium Publications

Written and Researched
by
Miriam Harrison & Shirley Alexander

ISBN 1 873877 29 3

Layout & Design
Nicholas Reardon

Drawings by
Peter T. Reardon & Caroline Alexander

Maps by Shirley Alexander & Andy Green
Photos by Miriam Harrison & Rupert Southcote

Reproduction of old prints by kind permission of
Cirencester Bingham Library

Printed by
In2Print Ltd, Cheltenham.

The Cirencester Experience
Roman Corinium "The Capital of the Cotswolds"

The ancient market town of Cirencester, situated in the south-eastern corner of the Cotswolds and just 90 miles, 145 kilometres, from our capital city, London, is steeped in history. It has been many things in its past. From a ford, a place to cross the river, it became a Roman fort and under Roman rule the fort grew into a city; the city of Corinium. In the whole of Britain only London was larger than Corinium or Cirencester as it is known today. In the 4th Century Britain was divided into four separate provinces and Cirencester's early importance was established by becoming became the capital of Britannia Prima, one of the four provinces. In the post Roman era the city became the scene of many royal disputes. In early Saxon times many fierce territorial battles ensued since the warring kingdoms seemed unable to agree the limits of their conquests.

One legendary tale, according to medieval writers, describes the besieging and burning of Cirencester in AD 586 in this manner:

The aggressor tied "to the feet of sparrow's which hys people had caught certain clewes of thred or matches finely wrought and tempered ready to take fire so that the sparrow's being suffered to go out of hand flew into the towne to lodge themselves within the nestes which they had made in stackes of corne or eaves of houses, so that the towne was thereby set on fire, and then the Brytones issuing forth fought with their enemies," and were overcome and discomforted.

It became known as " The City of Sparrows ".

Cirencester remained in the hands of the Wessex until merging into the Kingdom of England in AD 827.

The earliest mention of a trading market in Cirencester is in the Domesday Book of 1086. The wool trade began in Saxon times when Cirencester merchants exported to Flanders large quantities of wool which they exchanged for manufactured woollen goods. Confirmation of a grant of fairs by King John in 1216 and again by King Henry III in 1243 - 1248 emphasises the importance of the market. Cirencester's next important stage of development started in the post Norman era, the heyday of the wool trade. This step came about when several merchants of Amien settled in Cirencester as dealers of wool. However it was not until 1331 when Edward III invited weavers, dyers and fullers from Flanders to live in England, also granting them protection for trade, that a manufacturing base was established.

In Norman times the town was controlled by the mighty mitred Abbey of which much is written.

The 13th and 14th centuries brought irksome restrictions on the trade, by means of the staple. Staple goods produced in England, wool being by far the greatest, were to be sold only in designated places and caused much difficulty.

The 15th and 16th centuries were times of much growth. The Court Rolls of the 16th century all testify to the importance of the town. The numerous inns around the town attracted many visitors through their portals. Daniel Defoe wrote, around 1700:

"Cirencester is still a very good town, populous and rich, full of clothiers, and driving a great trade in wool. The vast quantities sold here are almost incredible . . . . They talk of 5000 packs a year"

In 1712 Cirencester had the largest wool market in the country, held in the Boothall.

In 1800 the historian Rudder says:

" . . . . the principal street was so thronged with wool wagons about forty years ago that it was difficult for other carriages to pass."

But wool dealers undermined the market by buying the wool directly from the local farmhouses. The market did not recover from this setback and indeed these dealers brought about its demise. The Corn Hall now stands on the former Boothall site.

During the nineteenth and twentieth centuries many alterations both good and not so good have taken place. Today Cirencester, so full of character, is the small market town you are about to see, but you may feel you are taking a trip back in time.

Point 1.
Corinium Gate and Plaque.

Open the book to find the centrefold map and the quiz. Locate the starting point and follow "The Cirencester Experience" circular walk.

On leaving the Beeches car park, cross directly over London Road to Corinium Gate on the right-hand side. At this point follow the wall to the right and look for a most interesting plaque high on the wall. It was erected by the Cirencester Civic Society and reads:

"On this site stood the north-east gate of Roman Corinium where the Fosse Way from Lincoln and Akeman Street from Verulamium (St Albans) entered the town. Excavation in 1960 revealed a gate 30 m wide with flanking towers and a dual carriage way of cobbled streets. The River Churn was diverted to flow just outside the town wall".

As you enter into Corinium Gate continue on the right-hand side, until you come to a small bridge with an iron railing on the right side and walk over it. Follow the path over the second bridge and enter the historic Abbey Grounds.

Point 2.
The Abbey Grounds and The Roman Wall.

Roman Wall - Cirencester

Here is the first piece of Roman history. A section of the Roman defence is visible behind the bank on the right, showing structural evidence of a military installation in Cirencester. Follow the signs to reach the exposed remains of the Roman wall. The wall was restored between 1967 and 1972. Do look at the informative map at this site. Ponder a little about the town's Roman history. At the time of the Roman conquest in AD 43, Britain's economy was based on the land and the population mainly lived on the farms. The Romans encouraged the local people to work with them and continue the thriving agricultural system for their mutual benefit, albeit under Roman rule. The Romans eventually brought peace, wealth and prosperity to the country.

Return to the pathway with the lake in view. Follow the path over the bridge, past many varieties of mature trees, until you reach the site of the Abbey of St Mary. The Abbey Grounds, now a park, stretching from the Gloucester Road to the Church yard of St John the Baptist, was once the Abbot's garden and the lake was his fish pond. While you are enjoying the beauty and tranquillity of the grounds it may enhance your enjoyment still further by reading a little of the history of the Abbey as you proceed toward the Abbey site.

The enormous power of the Abbey began when Henry I commenced the enlargement and restoration of the Church of the secular canons, in 1117. Some fourteen years later the granting of a charter, by this same Henry, transferred privileges of power and position from the Secular Canons to the Canons of Augustine whom he then placed into the new monastery. The Abbey was dedicated on 16th November 1176 to the patron saints of St Mary and St James in the presence of Henry II, grandson of the founder. Having already received gifts of lands, successive monarchs added still more lands, tax free privileges and wealth to the Abbey. Tax records show that Cirencester Abbey was the richest Augustinian House in the country. It is little wonder that the Abbey of St Mary was accused of being too powerful and frequently disregarding the rights of those less powerful than themselves. Over the next three centuries the townsmen quite often felt compelled to document the struggle between Abbey and town. A particular example of this kind of grievance was documented in 1222 when Henry III granted the Abbot the right to have his own gallows. Accordingly when wrongdoers were hung their goods and chattels became the property of the Abbot. A rather daring local landowner, Elias Giffard of Brimpsfield, erected his own gallows in order to reap similar benefits and swiftly evoked the anger and might of the Abbey. The powerful Abbey became mitred in 1416 allowing similar privileges to those held by a cathedral. Out of twenty-eight mitred Abbeys in the whole of England, Gloucestershire lay claim to six of them. This gave rise to the saying *"As sure as God is in Gloucestershire."* However the Abbey's days were drawing to an end, and in 1534, King Henry VIII declared himself to be supreme head of the Church of England and it became treason to say otherwise. The abolition of the monasteries returned money to the Crown and Cirencester's St Mary's Abbey finally surrendered to the King's commissioners on the 31st December 1539. The Abbey was demolished and the site was eventually sold by Elizabeth I to her physician Dr Richard Masters in 1564 for the sum of £59 16s 3d and remained in the family until the 1960's. Elizabeth I gave Dr Masters her mother's cup, known as the Anne Boleyn Cup. It can now be seen in the Church and is a highly prized part of Cirencester's history.

Point 3. The Abbey of St Mary site.

The Abbey of St Mary site

There is a plinth with a plan of the Abbey on the top to assist your imagination. Stones set in the grass mark the shape and boundaries of part of the Abbey. The semicircular balustrading by the site of the Abbey allows a good vantage point to appreciate the beautiful grounds. The panoramic view of the trees spreading their branches across the swathe of green taking the eye onward to the lake ever bobbing with wildfowl, offers a tranquil haven so close to the bustle of the town. With the semicircular balustrading on your left, walk up to the crossed paths and turn right. On your right you will see arched yew hedges and further boundaries of the abbey marked out in stones. Walk on through the gate and facing you is the high cross and the damaged Cedar tree.

Point 4.
The High Cross and West Market Place

The medieval High Cross was the principal cross and one of six which were scattered around the town. It once stood for many years at the head of the Market Place outside the former Ram Inn. When the Ram Inn was demolished the Medieval High Cross was moved to Lord Bathurst's estate but returned to its present position by the Parish Church in 1927. The importance of the High Cross was clearly seen as after the civil war and the execution of King Charles I, the monarchy and the House of Lords was abolished. In the following eleven years while England was a republic under Oliver Cromwell banns of marriage were read out at the High Cross on three market days and marriages were conducted there by a Justice of the Peace. Samuel Rudder writes in his "New History of Gloucestershire" in 1779:

Note that the reason where fore here wanteth severall yeares and some several months for weddings at this time the rump parliament sett forth an Act that all banns should be published three severall market dayes at the High Cross, and after such Publisheings the partnerss to bee married by Justice of the Peace, soe there was but little to be done in Churches, the said parliament all consisting of Anabaptists and Independents.

Across the road, the Crown, the hostelry on the corner, was a staging inn in the eighteenth century. The stage coaches known as "flying machines" left for journeys to London. The "True Briton" left the Crown at 6.00a.m. on Sundays, Wednesdays and Fridays. From the Ram Inn the "Safety Briton" left at 7.00a.m. on Tuesdays, Thursdays and Saturdays. With the introduction of turnpike roads around the 1720s the journey to the metropolis could be completed in a single day.

Point 5.
The Parish Church of St John the Baptist.

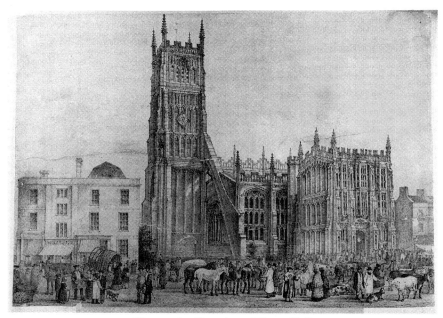

Cirencester Church and Town Hall

Before going into the Church, take a look at the tower and its surprisingly huge buttresses from the outside. The tower was begun around 1400 , just after the rebellion of the earls mentioned in Shakespeare's King Richard II, Act V scene 6:

Kind Uncle York the latest news we hear
Is that the rebels have consumed with fire
Our town of Cicester in Gloucestershire

The next news is, I have to London sent
The heads of Salisbury, Spencer, Blunt and Kent.

The townspeople of Cirencester beheaded the Earls of Kent and Salisbury. King Henry IV felt they should be rewarded for their services to the Crown and granted the town's men a charter which partially released them from the control of the Abbot.

The men and women of Cirencester were the beneficiaries in this manner:

For the men: four does in season out of his forest of Bredon and one hogshead of wine out of his port of Bristol.
For the women: six bucks in right season and one hogshead of wine out of the same port.

Finally, the granting of the rebel's goods to the townspeople enabled them to build the church tower. The original plan had been for a spire on top of the tower but the foundations, in Gosditch Street, proved inadequate to take the weight. The ditch close by, often frequented by geese, and giving rise to the name Gosditch (Gooseditch) was prone to flooding making the whole area unstable and so huge buttresses were erected to support the structure. What a pity the builders realised about subsidence or we may have been famous the world over for the leaning spire of Cirencester!

Enter the Parish Church from the entrance in the Market Place. It is open daily and on Sundays except during services. The magnificent porch, built for the Abbey in 1500 in the perpendicular style, is unique in the country. The great porch opening on to the market place was built about 1500 although it provided the church with a handsome porch it was in fact a secular building designed to provide a meeting place where legal and other business transactions could take place. At the dissolution of the Abbey in 1539 the chamber above the porch became the Town Hall by which name it is still known. In 1672 the Town Hall became the property of the Church which, in return, accepted the responsibility for its upkeep, but it was still used for secular purposes and the crypt below and the ground floor were used a wine store. Somewhat weather-worn figures on the porch exterior are extremely interesting *"pourtraying the social life and customs of three or four centuries since"* adorn the base of the battlements.

Enter the church through its impressive portals. The church is rich in historical interest.

On the East wall is the silver gilt cup which once belonged to King Henry VIII's second wife, Anne Boleyn. This important cup was made in 1532, two years before her death, and it features her personal badge, a falcon holding a sceptre with a rose tree. The safe housing is set into the stone work of a pillar and the cup can be viewed through the glass front.

The Anne Boleyn Cup

The pre-Reformation wine glass pulpit, dating from the 15th Century, is beautifully worked in open stone tracery and was redecorated in the 19th Century, some of the colour still remains. The nave of the church is lofty and impressive and early English in style. The splendid font was found in the Abbey Grounds, used as a flower pot, sometime in the 15th Century.

St Catherine's Chapel has a beautiful fan-vaulted ceiling; the roof had to be raised to accommodate it. Look at the wooden rerodos which show St Catherine with a wheel; this was carved in Oberammegau. St Cathrine was tied to a wheel and burnt. This is the origin of the "Catherine wheel" firework we set fire to, and watch spinning round, on November the fifth each year. The bosses show the Abbot's mitre and his initials, J H; and the date, 1508. On a section of the wall you will see pomegranates painted in a deep red colour; it is said they represent the seeds of life. Also you will see St Christopher carrying the Christ Child.

The archway which leads through into the Lady Chapel was once the outside door to the Abbey. The Lady Chapel has a lovely carved ceiling which includes a "Tom and Jerry", cat and mouse confrontation. Note the "squints" or hagioscopes, these are interesting openings in the wall allowing sight of the alters.

There was a time when all the windows of the Church were stained glass but they became sadly neglected. In 1642 Charles I's nephew, Prince Rupert, the dashing cavalry commander, lay siege to Cirencester, imprisoning more than a thousand men in the Church. It is said that they were treated with much cruelty. Relatives of Prince Rupert's prisoners threw food into the Church, through the windows, breaking a number of them. In the 18th Century the fragmented pieces were collected together and put into the great east and west windows; this was done by Samuel Lysons. The glass that was not used was crated and stored. In 1890 some of the glass was discarded into a ditch near the Cirencester-Kemble railway line. Only one case survived and in the late 1920s it was set by F.C. Eden into the window in the south sanctuary wall.

It is possible to take some brass rubbings in the church; a corner is set aside for this purpose. Children who are supervised by accompanying adults are welcomed. Enquire at the shop in the church. Paper and crayons are either supplied at the church or can be bought at the Cornerstone church shop.

In this outstanding Parish Church there is still so much more to enjoy and there are many informative books available. Explore the church at your leisure.

Point 6. Castle Street.

On leaving the church, turn right and cross over West Market Place at the narrow pedestrian crossing. Now cross over into Castle Street to the left-hand side. From this position look down Castle Street to the Lloyds Bank building, described by David Verey as "the best example of Palladian architecture in the town". It is the most elaborate of all the classical buildings in the town with its Ionic and Corinthian columns. Now a bank, it was originally built as a home for a wealthy wool-merchant and his family. Admire the late Victorian block, numbers 2 to 12, running from the corner of Castle Street down to the Post Office; it was completed in 1897 and the dates are on the rainwater heads. Do look up to the first floor to see the beautiful oriel window with a fine doorway beneath. Castle Street is named after the castle which stood in the vicinity. The ill-fated castle was sacked in 1142 but it was rebuilt soon after and demolished by order of Henry III in 1216.

Walk along past the "The Black Horse" public house, and cross over Castle Street past Lloyds Bank, into Silver Street. Look back at the street with its fine Cotswold-style gabled roof line. Continue on to the end of Silver Street and cross over to the Corinium Museum.

Point 7.
The Corinium Museum, Park Street.

The Corinium Museum houses a wide range of local artefacts from Roman times onwards and is well worth a visit if you have time. This important Roman collection surpasses many other large town and city museums.

The wool trade and other agricultural history is also displayed here. The entry charge to see this fine collection is very reasonable. Come out of the museum and turn right, walk down Park Street and facing you is what is said to be the highest yew hedge in England. Behind the high wall and hedge sits the Bathhurst estate. Continue walking, on the museum side of the road, towards Cecily Hill.

Point 8. Cecily Hill.

You will need to cross over the road to reach Cecily Hill. The bridge at the foot of the hill was called "Gunstoole" and was probable the site of the town's ducking stool as its name is a medieval corruption. Until 1854 the stream was open and used as a watering place for horses. The first building on the right is a Tontine terrace built by Thomas Bayley Howell in the classical style and it was inherited though the tontine by the third Earl Bathurst. A tontine being a form of annuity by which the shares of the sub-scribers to the building who die are added to the profits shared by the sur-vivors. The last survivor being the benefactor. Look across the road at number 5: this 17th Century house is possibly on the site of St. Cecilia's Chapel. The gothic bay windows were a later addition. Number 32 is a square 18th century house in the classical style and The Old Dolphin is a mellow-fronted house,

Cecily Hill Barracks

worthy of a look. Number 38 has the date 1909 nestling in the unusually carved wooden window bow and the letters W.H.S; note also the door frame. Number 40 and 42 form a single house with wings which was built in the 18th Century. On the other side of the road are many different architectural styles. Number 9 has mullion and transom windows and was built the 17th Century; number 27 also has mullion windows. All of these styles are brought together in harmony by of the use of Cotswold stone. The Old Barracks also known as the Armoury, at the top of Cecily Hill on the right, was constructed in 1856/7 in rusticated stone with castellations. It housed the North Gloucestershire Militia and later it was used for the 4th Battalion of the Glo'ster regiment for their annual training.

Here you take the 1st optional spur if time and energy allows, or continue on to point 9 on the map.

1st Optional Spur.
The seat of Earl Bathurst: Cirencester Park.

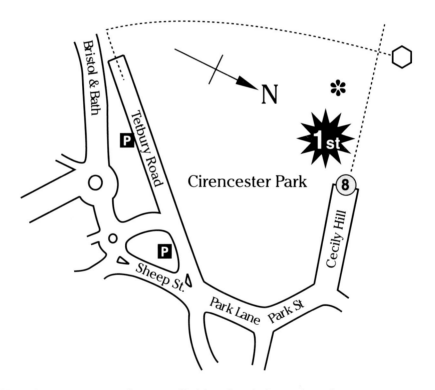

The short suggested route, linking back into the circular walk, is designed to give you a taste of the pleasure of perambulating here. There are many longer walks, with much of interest to see, for other occasions. Earl Bathurst generously opens the grounds between 8.00a.m. and dusk but picnicking is not allowed in the park. The Broad Ride stretches for 5 miles, 8 kilometres and extends to Sapperton and its lovely valley. On each side of the ride, the magnificent mature trees form the longest avenue in the country. As you walk up the rise, look back to see the wonderful view of the church from this vantage point. This breathtaking landscape you see before you is almost certainly guaranteed to lift the spirits. Along the Broad Ride a path crosses and if you glance to your right you will see the Hexagon, a summer house made of stone. Turn to the left and enjoy this part of the tranquil parkland walk. This short route brings you out onto the Bristol Road. Turn left into town. The path soon joins the truncated Tetbury Road, once the main road into town from the south. The grounds of the old cattle market can be seen on the right. Looking ahead to the bottom of Castle Street the old Police Station and Magistrate's Courts building commands the corner. Continue to walk beside the high hedge in Park Lane noting the old Grammar School House. The school was founded in 1457 by the Bishop of Lincoln. The building has undergone many alterations over the years and ceased to be a school in 1881. Return to Cecily Hill. You have now returned to the main circular walk.

Point 9. Coxwell Street.

From Cecily Hill cross over Thomas Street and into Coxwell Street. Coxwell Street, formally Abbots Street, was named after a wealthy family who lived in Coxwell Court. This house is now known as " The Woolgathers" and can be seen on the right as you enter the street. This area of the town has remained almost unchanged for three hundred years. Further down on the right is number 51, a large and imposing three-storey house with a magnificent façade and the mullion and transom windows which are a feature of the town. On the right-hand side of the street is the Baptist Church and almost opposite on the left is number 10, once the home of the lawyer, John Plot. The house has a Renaissance doorway with keystone and cornice. On the door case the old style letters I P, representing his initials, and the date 1640 are engraved. John Plot was a Royalist but his house was still ransacked by Prince Rupert's soldiers.

① Corinium Gate is now the name standing on a site of Roman fame. This _ _ _ _ _ _ will the facts proclaim.

ANSWER _____

② Upon entering the Abbey Grounds, what lies under the grassy bank?

ANSWER _____

③ Could this be a fishy question. What is it?

ANSWER _____

④ The cedar tree sustained a loss, but thankfully they saved the _ _ _ _ _ ?

ANSWER _____

⑤ In which of the chapels inside the church will you find Tom and Jerry?

ANSWER _____

⑥ Could this be a watering hole for animals or people, or even a sign of affluence?

ANSWER _____

⑦ Behind these pillars lay a lot of the town's history. Where are we?

ANSWER _____

⑧ Now we are in Cecily Hill, mammal or fish - that's your skill. What is it?

ANSWER _____

⑨ This house could spin a yarn or two. Name the house.

ANSWER _____

Above this door I P is what you see, John Plot lived here. Date above the door?

ANSWER _____

⑩ For Thomas Street we now shall make and find a place to shiver and shake. What house and the date?

ANSWER _____

John Wesley preached here in 1787. Did his words weave a message of hope ? Name the building?

ANSWER _____

MAF

KEY
❋ Park
✝ Church
ℹ Information
🅿 Car Park
🆃 Toilet

Sheep S

🅿

🅿
Brewe
Yard
3rd 🆃

Cricklade Stree

Lewis

Sth. Way Nth Way

🅿 🆃

Lane

18

Dyer St

Victoria Road

London Road

Purley Road

START 🆃

Beeches
Car Park 🅿

Beeches Road

London & Swindon

QUIZ

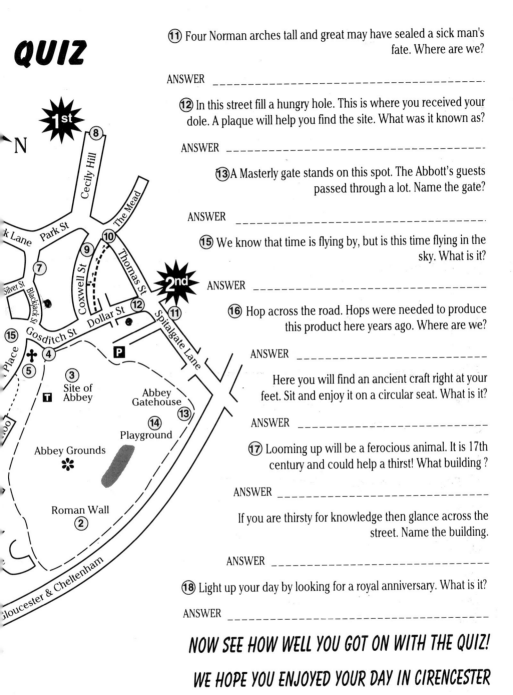

⑪ Four Norman arches tall and great may have sealed a sick man's fate. Where are we?

ANSWER _____

⑫ In this street fill a hungry hole. This is where you received your dole. A plaque will help you find the site. What was it known as?

ANSWER _____

⑬ A Masterly gate stands on this spot. The Abbott's guests passed through a lot. Name the gate?

ANSWER _____

⑮ We know that time is flying by, but is this time flying in the sky. What is it?

ANSWER _____

⑯ Hop across the road. Hops were needed to produce this product here years ago. Where are we?

ANSWER _____

Here you will find an ancient craft right at your feet. Sit and enjoy it on a circular seat. What is it?

ANSWER _____

⑰ Looming up will be a ferocious animal. It is 17th century and could help a thirst! What building ?

ANSWER _____

If you are thirsty for knowledge then glance across the street. Name the building.

ANSWER _____

⑱ Light up your day by looking for a royal anniversary. What is it?

ANSWER _____

NOW SEE HOW WELL YOU GOT ON WITH THE QUIZ!

WE HOPE YOU ENJOYED YOUR DAY IN CIRENCESTER

Walk back along Coxwell Street, past St Clement's Walk and turn right opposite number 51 into St Clement's Walk and take the path to the left as indicated by the arrows on the map into Thomas Street. Turn right.

Point 10. Thomas Street.

Weavers' Hall

Thomas Street takes its name from St Thomas's Hospital, now known as Weavers' Hall, and dedicated to St Thomas a Becket. The building on the right is the Friends Meeting House, where the Quakers meet. It was built in 1673 and has been in continuous use by the Friends ever since. On the other side of the road is the Salvation Army Temple built in 1846 and a little further down stands the aforementioned historic Weavers' Hall. The Weavers' Hall, with it's weather-worn carving above the door, was built by Sir William Nottingham, Attorney General to Edward IV and a town benefactor. The building was left in trust for the "for the benefit of four poor men". Sir William did not forget their financial needs since he left a sum of money to be distributed to them weekly. The Weavers' Hall is thought to be the oldest secular building in Cirencester. John Wesley preached there in 1787. At the end of Thomas Street turn left into Dollar Street. Continue along to Gloucester Street.

Here you take the next optional spur or continue onto point 11 on the map.

2nd Optional Spur.
The Barton Mill and River Churn.

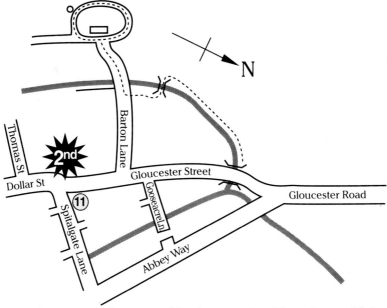

Walk into Gloucester Street and look up to the blue plaque high up on the wall of the old school house. The Blue School gave 20 boys and 20 girls a basic Christian education and the Yellow school, endowed by Rebecca Powell, clothed and educated 40 boys and 20 girls. The dress of both of the schools was similar to other chari-ty schools founded around the beginning of the eighteenth century. Opposite the school house is number 2, notable for the finely carved stone mullions and two blocked in doorways and one first floor window also blocked. Look also at the end of the building.

A little further down on the right is a regency style building housing Corinium Court Hotel, do look through the archway into their pretty courtyard. Barton Hall is on the left and next is number 33, a timber-framed building with a plinth of very large stones under the windows said to have come from the Abbey. While most of the stone from the demolished Abbey was carted away a small amount still remains in the town. Cross over Barton Lane. On this corner was St Lawrence's Hospital, founded by Edith Biset, Lady of Wiggold, as a leper hospital. Later it was taken over by the Abbey and used as an almshouse. Many small Cotswold style cottages adorn this old street which was once the main road to Gloucester out of the town.

On the corner of Gooseacre Lane stands the Nelson Arms. Look out on the left for "Post Box Cottage", number 97 and on the right-hand side of the road is another charming terrace; numbers 82, 84 and 86. Number 105 has a fine moulded stone door case and is dated 1679 with the initials B B I. Further down on the left is a Tudor-style house built in 1906 and tucked into a corner on the left is The Old House, number 187.

Cross over the road and squeeze through a narrow gap in the wall to look at the River Churn and the start of the Mill Pound by the sluice gate foot bridge. Return and cross over the bridge, turn left and walk along the mill stream beside the fields enjoying the pastoral stillness. This area is known as The Barton. Cross over the bridge, walk to the end of the path and turn right. Take the road ahead of you. over the speed ramps. It is just a few metres is another gated entrance into Cirencester Park. The park is open from 8.00a.m. until dusk or as indicated on the notice board on the left. The old Barton Mill stood in this vicinity, but sadly burned down in 1923. Go through the park entrance where "The Great Barn" greets the eye. Next bear left for a short way and then right along the roadway. Soon you will espy the Barton Dove Cote. Continue on following the way until you reach the fine Barton House. Walking past low roofed Cotswold stone buildings, you will soon have completed the route and be back at the park entrance. Retrace your steps as a far as the pathway over the bridge and look over to the right to see another view of the Barracks. Walk down Barton Lane to Gloucester Street past

the large commercial building and little cottages on the left and Powell's School playing fields on the right. Cross over Gloucester Street and return to point 11 on the map noting on the way the shadowy earlier roof line of the cottage next to Barton Hall. You are now back on the circular walk.

Point 11. The hospital of St John the Evangelist.

Hospital of St John the Evangelist

The Norman arcade is all that is left of the hospital of St. John the Evangelist, endowed by Henry I and later by Henry II. The original meaning of the word hospital did not have the same connotations as the modern use of the word. In this time it meant a home for poor families, the elderly, infirm and the destitute. Spitalgate Lane, is a corruption of Hospital Gate and refers to the name of the lane in which the hospital of St John stands. This area had a reputation for being rat infested and was also known as "raton-rewe" or rotton-row. A plaque under the arches gives information about this former hospital. Cross the road and walk back into Dollar Street.

Point 12.   Dollar Street.

The name Dollar is a corruption of dole-hall or possibly dole-hole, the place where charitable gifts were "doled out" from the Abbot to the poor and needy town's people and travellers. A field or meadow nearby belonging to the monastery, called the dole-mead, provided the income to finance the giving of alms. There are many examples of fine architecture in Dollar Street. Dollar Street House was built by the lawyer Joseph Pitt and has a doorway with Ionic portico.   Number 30, Park House, is a three-storey building with elliptical arched windows and a rainwater head dated 1725. Next to the old Abbey wall is a row of houses, numbers 2 to 8, dating from the 17th Century; these are stone houses with gables. Number 1 Dollar Street is now Cirencester Vicarage and next door at number 3 there is a small book shop also housing a tiny cafe. The 19th Century house across the small road is barge board fronted with first floor niches containing female figures. Walk though the archway of number 16, set back a little from the road. This is the site of the former western entrance gate to the Abbey, known as Dole-Hall Gate or Almery, but first do take the time to read the plaque on the way as it explains about the dole. Cross the road behind number 16, walk through the Abbey Grounds Car Park and back into the Abbey Grounds. Turn left and walk along to the gate house of the Abbey.

Point 13. The Abbey Gate-house and northern entrance to the Abbey Grounds.

This Abbey Gate House is known as Spitalgate as it was the entrance to the Abbey's Hospitium, a building set aside for the accommodation and entertainment of strangers.

In the archway there is a plaque commemorating the town receiving the gift of the Abbey Gate House from the Chester-Master family, descendants of Dr Masters who purchased the property from Elizabeth I. The words read as follows:

The 12th Century Gate House, the only surviving building of the Great Augustian Abbey of St Mary, was one of the entrances to the precincts of the monastery until it's dissolution in 1539.

Purchased from Queen Elizabeth 1 by Dr Richard Master, physician to the Queen. The Abbey site remained in the ownership of his descendants until 1964 when the Gate House was presented to Cirencester in memory of the late Col. W.A.Chester-Master by his family.

Spitalgate - Cirencester

Point 14.   The Recreation Area.

If you have children you may wish to use the recreation area; the swings and other recreational equipment have sand underfoot for safety. After the swings proceed along the path past points 3 and 4 to point 15.

Point 15. The Market Place.

The Old Market Place

The market held in the town was first described in the Domesday book of 1086 as the "new market", and its modern counterpart can still be enjoyed on Mondays and Fridays. In the 19th Century three small streets known as Shoe Lane, Butter Row and Botchers Row stood at the top of the Market Place. These rows, filled the road and the buildings almost touched the church's porch. At the head of the square stood the High Cross and at the other end a group of houses were known as the "Shambles". They were all purchased and finally demolished by 1830 to comply with a charter passed for the purpose of implementing town improvements. These included such things as cleansing, drainage, paving and lighting. The money was raised from the sale of the common land at Watermoor.

The Market Place was once the home of "The Mop Fair", one of many fairs for the hiring of farm and domestic servants up and down the country. This fair occurred on the Mondays before and after October 11th, but if that day fell on a Monday there were three "mops". The hiring function moved to the Corn Hall in 1862.

Before the 1920's when pitches could be booked, showmen wanting the best pitch would wait at the edge of town until the church clock struck midnight. They would race down into town to claim their prime position. The modern sideshows and fairground rides continued in the Market Place until the 1960s when "The Mop Fair" moved to its present position in the Forum Car Park.

There is a wealth of architectural detail in the Market Place. An excellent vantage point to view these fine buildings is from the Parish Church porch-way. An artist's palette of orange, pink, beige, grey and natural stone sweep the Market Place to the left and right. The black and white timbered Fleece Hotel, greatly complements the scene. Cast your eye high to note the rakish angles of the roof lines and chimneys nestling in such harmony one with another. Nearest to the church the facades above the shop fronts are Georgian and worthy of perusal. A walkway between the south porch of the Church and these buildings gives access to the churchyard and a fine view of these houses from the rear. Look for the Waterloo passage said to have taken its name from a chair bearing the name Waterloo and kept at location. It was used for transporting ladies to and from evening parties and entertainment.

Across the wide Market Square the Italinate Corn Hall, is finished in cream ashlar. A craft market is held here on the 2nd and 4th Saturdays every month from 10.00a.m. to 4.30p.m. Next to the Corn Hall stands the Kings Head Hotel with its cream coloured stucco façade. Look up and note the unusual arched windows set below its roof line. A third classically-inspired building, with shops on the ground floor, is decorated with elegant stone swags and gives the Market Place grace and dignity.

Point 16.   The Brewery Arts Centre.

Turn into Cricklade Street by the Midland Bank opposite the church, cross over the road outside Woolworth's and go through the pedestrian way towards the Brewery Arts Centre. In the centre of the Brewery Yard is a courtyard edged with seating, and a replica of the Roman hare mosaic which was discovered in the

Beeches area of Cirencester and is now in the Corinium Museum. The nationally recognised craft centre, which comprises craft workshops, galleries, coffee shop, craft shop and an intimate theatre is housed in a converted Victorian brewery. Inside the various workshops many talented Cotswold artists have their wares for sale. This offers an opportunity to either enjoy looking at, or purchase, these unique pieces of art and craft. A cafe is situated behind the craft shops at the top of a fight of wooden steps. Return to Cricklade Street.

At this point we offer you a 3rd optional spur or a continuation of the circular walk. Should you choose to continue with the circular walk return to the Market Place by turning left and turn right into the Market Place. Follow the road down, past the Kings Head, to the Bear Inn, point 17 on the map.

3rd Optional Spur.

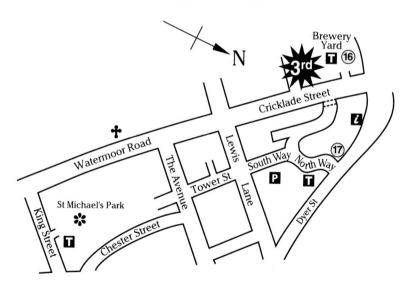

If you choose to take this optional spur, turn right on your return to Cricklade Street and walk away from the church. The shops here are the main feature of the street because whatever beautiful architecture once graced this area has long gone and has been replaced by modern buildings. Towards the end of the street there are some pleasant examples of gable fronted and mullion windowed, Cotswold-style buildings. Cross at the cross-roads at the bottom of Cricklade Street into Watermoor Road.

In the 12th Century this area was known as "The Moor" indicating an area of uncultivated or common land. This poorly drained land was liable to flooding due to its low-lying position near to the River Churn. Later the area became known as Watermoor, which was, as the name suggests, waterlogged. The first road through was called Watery Lane. On the left are the Bowly Almshouses. Christopher Bowly was a Quaker and a town benefactor. On the right by the first entrance are the remains of two Roman columns. A disused water pump stands close by a row known as Bowly's Cottages and a little further down the road is a small peaceful cemetery.

Take the first turning to the left into the road known as The Avenue. At the next crossroad turn to the right to see, marked out in light coloured cement on the surface of the road, the outline of the altar of the Roman Basilica. Do take time to read the interesting plaque. The Basilica described as a Cathedral-like building was a great aisled hall about 100 metres long and 24 metres wide with an arched or domed recess at one end. From the south-east side of this great hall led many further rooms used for the purposes of administration. Taxes were collected from here and legal disputes settled. Petty crimes would also have been dealt with here. On the north-west side of the great hall was the forum. The Masonic hall, on the right, with its beautiful single Venetian window, stands on part of the original Roman site. Continue along the side road into St Michael's Park.

St Michael's Park is the most recently planned park in Cirencester and has two play areas for children, crazy golf, a putting green, tennis courts and large areas of grass to picnic and play on. When you have enjoyed time here and feel refreshed retrace your steps to the entrance and enjoy this different view of the church tower. Walking towards the Church, cross The Avenue and continue along

Tower Street. The road aligns directly to the tower of the parish church. Note the five ancient gate piers on your right. Cross over Lewis Lane into South Way and North Way and stop to see the plaque set into the wall on your left. It reads:

Here is the crossing of the two great Roman roads of Ermin Street and the Foss Way (already joined with Akeman Street). Corinium developed around this site.

Continue walking past the Forum car park, on your right, so named as it stand in the vicinity of the historic site of the old Roman forum. Although it cannot be seen any longer it is worthy of a brief description. The forum was a large open courtyard or piazza, measuring 108 metres by 68 metres, and used as a meeting place. Shops and offices stood on three sides of the courtyard. A covered colonnade was erected, on all sides, to protect the patrons from inclement weather. In the fourth century, whilst modifications were taking place, a mosaic was laid in the colonnade. Follow the road around to point 17 on the map, the Bear Inn. You have now returned to the circular walk.

Point 17. The Bear Inn.

The Bear Inn, on the left, is a 17th century timber framed building that was altered to make way for the Forum Car Park and the police station. Take time to look at the red information board situated on the Market Place side of the building. It reads;

This Inn which is believed to be the earliest coaching Inn in Cirencester and dates from early 14th Century, was extensively altered in recent times when North Way was built but still retains most of its original interior features. many of the beams which can be seen in the bars were taken from old sailing ships.

Cross over Dyer Street to view the old Bingham Library, with its oriel window over a castellated door, which was donated to the town by Daniel Bingham. He was a clerk with the Great Western

Railway who went to Holland to assist with their railways. He made his fortune, invested wisely and did not forget his home town. The trust he set up is still operating today. Other classical buildings grace Dyer Street; one impressive house has a Roman Doric doorway. A small arcade of shops called the Woolmarket can be reached by walking through the archway past the statue of a ram. On leaving this arcade turn left away from the Market Place and church. Some of Dyer Street has been rebuilt in modern style in reconstructed stone.

Point 18. Jubilee Lamp.

On the right side of the road, set in a small square and surrounded by trees, is the Jubilee Lamp. The Lamp was moved from its original site in Park Lane, where it stood outside the old police station, to its present site in Dyer Street following alteration to the road. The inscription reads:

This Lamp was erected by the inhabitants of Cirencester to commemorate the Silver Jubilee of his Majesty King George V, 1910 - 1935.

Continue down the road. Gloucester House, once the home of Rebecca Powell the philanthropist, is on the right. It is now an impressive office building and was once a furniture showroom. The old company name and business is written in mosaic and set into the pavement outside. Further down the road is the office of the Wilts and Gloucestershire Standard. Newspapers have been printed in Cirencester from as early as 1698. The "Standard" building is not so old it was built in the Tudor-style with overhanging floors in 1904.

Our walk is almost over. Go down to the bottom of Dyer Street on the right-hand side, cross the road, Lewis Lane and cross over Victoria Road, make your way back to the car park . On the way back up do look across the road at the "Wagon and Horses" a fine old Cotswold pub and at Oxford House with its fine classical lines.

The Wagon and Horses

Enter the car park through the footpath by the River Churn and return to the present century.

We leave you with the evocative words of this poem entitled:

A Capital Town

The clatter of chariots, the crackling of flame.
The fame of the fleeces, the Abbey's rich gain.
The Church with it's prisoners held by Rupert's cruel hand.-
Power of the Monarchs seizing money and land.
Granting of charters to better the town.
A Domesday named market of ancient renown.
Throughout a long history, Cicester shall affirm
It's the gem of the Cotswolds, inviting return.

M.H.

We hope you have enjoyed *The Cirencester Experience* and that you have discovered what this ancient market town has to offer the visitor.

Have you successfully completed the quiz? The answers can be found on page 36.

Please look for others in this series: *The Cheltenham Experience* and *The Burford Experience*. Available at Tourist Information Centres and at all good book shops.

Roman and Royal connections on the outskirts of Cirencester.

The Roman Amphitheatre is directly across town and sign posted. Beecham describes the amphitheatre as "...one of the most perfect examples of its kind in the kingdom". It was formed by using soil and refuse from the adjacent quarries to construct the embankments which enclosed the arena.. Amphitheatres in Britain were always earthwork structures. Thought to be 2nd Century AD the Cirencester amphitheatre held between eight and nine thousand people making it larger than any other in Britain. In the 18th Century the amphitheatre arena was used for bull-baiting giving rise to the popular local title of "The Bull Ring". The site has not been fully excavated but many bodies, believed to have been victims of gladiatorial combat were found when the ring road was constructed.

Three miles down the A419 towards Stroud is Peddington Polo Ground offering world-class polo. HRH Prince Charles plays here regularly. The polo ground is in Cirencester park and energetic walkers can reach it from Cecily Hill.

Take the A433, the Tetbury Road out of Cirencester and on the right-hand side you will see the internationally famous Royal Agricultural College. The college was granted the Royal Charter of incorporation by Queen Victoria in 1845. This conferred upon the proposed institution the title of "The Royal Agricultural College for teaching the science of agriculture, and the various sciences connected therewith, and practical application thereof to the cultivation of the soil and in the rearing and management of stock". The college building were opened on April 30th 1846 and by June one hundred students enrolled, the youngest being only fourteen years of age. The college still has royal connections today as Her Majesty Queen Elizabeth is patron and HRH Prince Charles is president of the college.

The town is surrounded by a plethora of beautiful Cotswold villages. Information is freely available at the Tourist Information Centre in the Market Place, Cirencester.

Gargoyle on Cirencester Church

Bibliography

Atkyns, Sir Robert.
The Ancient and Present State of Gloucestershire.
Originally published in 1712. Republished in 1974 by E.P.
Publishing in collaboration with Gloucestershire County Library.

Beecham, K.J.
History of Cirencester.
Originally published in 1887. Republished in 1978 by Alan Sutton
Ltd.

Darvill, Timothy and Gerrard, Christopher.
Cirencester: Town and Landscape.
Published in 1994 by Alan Sutton publishing Ltd.

Hill, Canon Rowland E.
Cirencester Parish Church An Account of its History and
Architecture.
Published in 1981 by The Friends of Cirencester Parish Church.

Reece, Richard and Catling, Christopher.
Cirencester: The Development and Buildings of a Cotswold Town.
A British Archaeological Report published in 1975.

Rudder, Samuel.
A New History of Gloucestershire.
Originally published in 1779. Republished in 1977 by Alan Sutton in
collaboration with Gloucestershire County Library.

Tomkins, Richard.
Street Names of Cirencester.
Published in 1987 by Red Brick Publishing.

Welsford, Jean.
Cirencester A History and Guide.
Published in 1987 by Alan Sutton Ltd.

Answers

to the

Cirencester Experience Quiz

1.	Plaque
2.	The remains of the Roman Wall.
3.	The lake or Abbot's fish pond.
4.	Cross.
5.	The Lady Chapel.
6.	The Black Horse.
7.	Corium Museum.
8.	A dolphin door knocker.
9.	The Woolgatherers.
	1640
10.	The Quaker Friends Meeting House. 1673
	The Weavers' Hall
11.	The hospital of St John the Evangelist, Spitalgate Lane.
12.	The Almery or Dole-hole
13.	Spitalgate
15.	The church clock.
16.	The Brewery Yard.
	The Hare Mosaic
17.	The Bear Inn
	Bingham House Library.
18.	The Jubilee Lamp.

Why not try a Cirencester Experience on Tape for only £3.95 plus postage

If you have enjoyed reading this book on Cirencester, you may be interested to know that you can purchase your very own personal guide to Cirencester's historic past, to play on a "Walkman" as you explore this wonderful town, or just sit back and listen to in the comfort of your own home or car, letting your mind be taken on a guided tour of Cirencester town and parks, each tape comes complete with booklet containing town map and fun quiz.

Narrated by Chris Harrison

Please send your cheque for £4.95 (£3.95 plus £1.00 postage and packing) to REARDON PUBLISHING 56, Upper Norwood St, Leckhampton, Cheltenham, Glos, GL53 0DU. tel: (01242) 231800